Thinking Sociologically

A Critical Thinking Activities Manual

SECOND EDITION

Josephine Ruggiero

Providence College

Allyn and Bacon

Boston · London · Toronto · Sydney · Tokyo · Singapore

This book is dedicated to the memory of my parents,
John and Elvira Ruggiero, who first gave me the opportunity
and the freedom to think sociologically,
and
to my husband, Helmut Reinhardt, who gives me the
encouragement and support which enables me to continue to do so.

TABLE of CONTENTS

OVERVIEW

Developing good critical thinking skills is important in thinking sociologically and in the roles we play in everyday life, including the role of consumer of large amounts of information from a variety of sources. When you learn to think critically, you will be better able, for example, to identify and challenge commonly held assumptions, use the sociological perspective to analyze important social issues, read the popular media with more insight, evaluate the adequacy and accuracy-- strengths and weaknesses-- of the evidence used to support an argument in order to reach a well-reasoned conclusion, have a better grasp of the complexity of causal relationships, and be able to recognize and draw out the implications/applications of theory and research for change.

This manual contains twelve short, related exercises, each concentrating on a single critical thinking skill. Each exercise usually begins with a brief explanation of the nature of the skill and a simple example drawn either from sociology or everyday life. Through a series of questions, you will be guided through a three-step process in which you will **think critically about an issue or problem**, (the cognitive section), **analyze the mental processes involved in thinking critically** (the metacognitive section), and either **transfer the skill to other issues/problems or expand on ideas developed earlier in the exercise** (the application section). The three sections of each exercise are, thus, entitled respectively: "Thinking Critically, "Thinking About Thinking" and "Applying What You Have Learned."

Although the goal of critical thinking may be to reach a well-reasoned conclusion or to solve a problem, it is important for you to become aware of the thinking processes which lead you to different conclusions or solutions. By thinking metacognitively, or consciously reflecting on the mental steps involved in each thinking skill, you can gain a deeper understanding of the important elements in critical thinking. You should then be better able to apply the critical thinking skills you develop to issues and problems you encounter in your studies and in everyday life.

I. IDENTIFYING ASSUMPTIONS

The models people use to explain how the world works and the positions they hold on issues-- such as capital punishment, welfare, day care for young children, and working mothers-- are based on assumptions. When you identify assumptions, you uncover the hidden reasons that often serve as the bases for an orientation, opinion, or action.

Assumptions are ideas that are "taken for granted" or accepted as true without proof or examination. For example, in order to do research, social scientists make certain assumptions about the social world, about human behavior, and about the nature of relationships. They assume that the social world-- like the natural world-- is orderly and regular, that social behavior is patterned, that cause and effect relationships can be established, and that, given sufficient time and effort, the relationships that exist can be observed and demonstrated.

Assumptions may be difficult to uncover either because they are not obvious or perhaps because they are buried far below our level of awareness. Nevertheless, spending the time to identify the hidden assumptions at the root of a particular model, opinion, or decision is well worth the effort. By learning to identify assumptions, you will be able to recognize and understand better what accounts for the principal differences between people who hold different theoretical orientations within a discipline-- such as, for example, between sociologists who are order theorists and those who are conflict theorists-- and across disciplinary boundaries-- such as, for example, between sociologists and psychologists.   Focusing on the latter, think for a moment about the units of analysis where these professionals place their attention and on the kinds of variables they use to explain behavior.   Sociologists focus their attention on the group or aggregate as the unit of analysis and on explanatory variables outside the person, that is, on the effects of social forces and structural variables on behavior.   Sociologists are concerned with understanding interaction.   Although some sociologists focus on the micro-level (small scale), many focus their analyses on the macro-level (big picture).   By contrast, psychologists focus on the individual as their principal unit of analysis.   Psychologists generally look for explanatory variables which are inside the person (i.e., attitudes, motivations, mental or emotional states, etc.) to explain a person's behavior.   Their emphasis, therefore, is on the micro level.

A.   **THINKING CRITICALLY**

The focus of this exercise is on both the process of identifying assumptions and on the particular assumptions identified. To identify an assumption, it is important to analyze a thought or action in order to pick out the idea on which it is founded.   Consider the following excerpts from the 8th edition of Eitzen and Zinn, In Conflict and Order, Understanding Society,[1] describing the order and conflict perspectives:

---

[1]
D. Stanley Eitzen and Maxine Baca Zinn.   In Conflict and Order, Understanding Society, 8th ed. Boston: Allyn and Bacon, 1998, pp. 52-55.

SOCIAL SYSTEMS: ORDER AND CONFLICT

One of the characteristics of societies-- the ex-
istence of segmentation-- is the basis of two pre-
vailing models of society. Every society is com-
posed of parts. This differentiation may result
from differences in age, race, sex, physical prow-
ess, wisdom, family background, wealth, organizational membership, type of work, or any other
characteristics considered to be salient by the
members. The fundamental question concerning
differentiation is this: What is the basic relationship among the parts of society?...

The Order Model

... Societies are viewed as social systems, com-
posed of interdependent parts that are linked
together into a boundary-maintaining whole. The
parts of the system are basically in harmony with
each other. The high degree of cooperation (and
social integration) is accomplished because there
is a high degree of consensus on societal goals
and on cultural values. Moreover, the different
parts of the system are assumed to need each other
because of complementary interests. Because the
primary social process is cooperation, and the
system is highly integrated, all social change is
gradual, adjustive, and reforming. Societies are
therefore basically stable units.

For order theorists, the central issue is: What
is the nature of the social bond?...

The Conflict Model

... The basic form of interaction is not cooperation but competition, which often leads to conflict. Because the individuals and groups of
society compete for advantage, the degree of
social integration is minimal and tenuous. Social
change results from the conflict among competing
groups and therefore tends to be drastic and
revolutionary. The ubiquitousness of conflict
results from the dissimilar goals and interests
of social groups. It is, moreover, a result of
social organization itself.

3

... the unity present in society is superficial because it results not from consensus but from coercion. The powerful, it is asserted, use force and fraud to keep society running smoothly, with benefits mostly accruing to those in power. (Eitzen and Baca Zinn 1998, pp. 52-55)

1.　Can you identify the principal assumptions about society on which the functionalist and the conflict theories rest?

ORDER Theory:

_____

_____

_____

_____

CONFLICT Theory:

_____

_____

_____

_____

2.　Suppose you just read a report which stated, among other findings, that full-time female workers still earn significantly less money than full-time male workers even when level of education completed and job prestige were the same (that is, "controlled") for both sexes. How would you explain such a finding from an order perspective? from a conflict perspective?

_____

_____

_____

_____

_____

B. **THINKING ABOUT THINKING**

3. Describe the thinking process you went through in
    trying to identify the assumptions held by order
    and conflict theorists in question 1.

    _____

    _____

    _____

    _____

4. Describe your thinking steps in answering question 2.

    _____

    _____

    _____

    _____

5. What advice would you give to another student about
    how to identify disciplinary or theoretical assump-
    tions?

    _____

    _____

    _____

    _____

5

C. **APPLYING WHAT YOU HAVE LEARNED**

    6.   You read recently that a society was discovered in the remote outreaches of the East Indies (Pacific Islands). Identify some social characteristics which you think members of this society might have. Now, look over your list. What assumption(s) did you make before you generated your list of social characteristics?

_____

_____

_____

_____

_____

_____

_____

II. UNDERSTANDING and USING the SOCIOLOGICAL PERSPECTIVE

Sociologists are trained in the "sociological perspective." This unique way of looking at human social behavior contains a number of assumptions about how social behavior and events should be examined. As you learned in Exercise I, an assumption is a <u>taken for granted</u> idea. The most basic assumption in the sociological perspective is that the individual and society are two sides of the same coin; that is, to understand behavior you must examine and interpret it in the context in which it occurs. This context has a social dimension as well as cultural, political, and economic ones.

The sociological perspective also includes the following related or other assumptions:

- focus on **social interaction**

- focus on the **group or aggregate** rather than on the individual level of analysis

- **look for patterns** in the behavior under examination

- look at **what people have in common** rather than at ways in which they are different

- recognize that **people tend to behave in fairly predictable ways** and that **identifying patterns** makes predictions on the aggregate level possible

- **take into account historical processes as they influence behavior;** recognize Mills' (1959) notion that human beings are the products as well as the producers of their times

- **look beneath the surface of common sense explanations to discover the true nature of an issue.** We call this sociology's debunking function.

7

- **look at the familiar in an objective, impartial way,** as though through the eyes of a stranger

- take a **cross-cultural or more global perspective** as needed to examine issues of interest to the sociologist; understand the variability of behavior patterns from one society to another and within complex, heterogeneous societies like the United States.

A. THINKING CRITICALLY

In recent years, we have become more aware of the issues of violence in families-- spousal/partner, child, and elder abuse-- both in American society and worldwide. Most people have a opinion about what constitutes child abuse, what the perpetrator(s) is (are) like, and why it happens. In this exercise you will be using a sociological perspective to define and analyze child abuse.

1. Using a sociological approach, **define child abuse.** Be as specific as possible.

    a. First, **identify the various dimensions of the concept.**

    _____

    _____

    _____

    _____

    b. Based on what you say above, **provide a good theoretical definition of child abuse.**

    _____

    _____

    _____

8

2. **Keeping in mind the assumptions of the sociological perspective,** describe how you think a sociologist would approach studying the topic of child abuse.

a. That is, what would she or he **focus on and/or emphasize** about his issue?

_____

_____

_____

_____

b. List FIVE **social** variables which you think sociologists would examine as predictors of (that is, to explain) child abuse:

a. _____

b. _____

c. _____

d. _____

e. _____

c. Show how you think EACH of these variables is related to child abuse by proposing a specific testable hypothesis (statement of relationship) between each above-named variable and child abuse.

In stating a causal hypothesis, treat child abuse as the Dependent Variable (the effect) and the other variables as Independent (a cause) in each hypothesis.   Each hypothesis should contain <u>one</u> proposed cause and <u>one</u> effect.   **Make each hypothesis directional.**

For example, suppose you focus on the **variable of age** as a predictor of child abuse. You might pose the following directional hypothesis:

Younger parents are more likely to abuse their children than are older parents.

Of course, to test this hypothesis, you need to 1) define exactly which ages fall into the "younger" and "older" categories and   2) col-

9

lect data on the variable of age as well as
child abuse for a sample of individuals.

Hypothesis #1: _____

_____

Hypothesis #2: _____

_____

Hypothesis #3: _____

_____

Hypothesis #4: _____

_____

Hypothesis #5: _____

_____

3. What distinguishes the way a **sociologist versus a
   psychologist** would examine the issue of child abuse?

_____

_____

_____

B.   **THINKING ABOUT THINKING**

4.   Describe the thinking steps you took to produce
     your definition of child abuse in question 1b.
     and your list of variables in question 2b of
     Part A.

_____

_____

_____

_____

_____

5.   What suggestions can you give other students about
     how to use the sociological perspective to think
     about social issues like spousal/partner abuse,
     date or acquaintance rape, or marijuana use among
     college students.

_____

_____

_____

_____

_____

C.   **APPLYING WHAT YOU HAVE LEARNED**

In a discussion about child abuse, a family member tells you

that, rather than being a widespread problem, child abuse is a

problem of the lower social classes.

6.   In light of what you have learned about the socio-
     logical perspective, how would you respond to this
     comment?

_____

_____

continue ...

11

_____

_____

7. Discuss the **sociological implications** for inter-
    ventions and their **likely success** in this area.

    a. That is, suppose you wanted to reduce the
        incidence of child abuse in American society,
        <u>what/who</u> would you <u>target for change</u>
        and <u>why</u>? Identify at least three targets
        and explain why you chose them.

1. _____

_____

_____

2. _____

_____

_____

3. _____

_____

_____

    b. Which of the interventions you identified should
        have the **highest priority**? Explain.

_____

_____

_____

    c. Specifically <u>how</u> would you advise bringing about
        this/these change(s)?

_____

_____

_____

d.   What else needs to be taken into account to
     improve the chances of success of your strategy?

_____

_____

_____

e.   What effect(s) do you think the efforts you
     described will have in the short term? In the
     long run? Explain you answer.

_____

_____

_____

_____

III. **COMPARING and CONTRASTING**

The act of comparing and contrasting can be a powerful thinking tool because it can help you discover things that you might
not otherwise notice and it can lead to sound decision making.
When you <u>compare</u> ideas, issues, or events, you note their similarities or common characteristics as well as their differences.
When you <u>contrast</u>, you compare ideas, issues or events **in order
to emphasize their differences.** When very similar things are
compared and contrasted, previously unseen patterns may be revealed.
For example, in the first critical thinking exercise, you identified the assumptions of the Functionalist and Conflict perspectives.
These two theories are often **compared as to their their focus** (e.g.,
both are macro or societal level) and **contrasted as to their
assumptions about society** (e.g., the former views the social world
as a basically orderly place whereas proponents of the latter see
society as in a constant state of conflict and change).

Let's look at another example in more detail. Imagine that
you are a young, married college graduate. You and your spouse are
expecting your first child. You have both worked for several years
since finishing college and are in a position to buy a really nice
new car. You are leaning towards buying a sports coupe which seats
four. However, your spouse thinks that it makes more sense to purchase a minivan because your family's needs are growing.

You have looked over <u>Consumer Reports' Guide to New Cars</u>.
You been also been reading auto advertisements in your local news-
paper for the last several weeks and have made a few visits to local
dealerships to look at various vehicles and prices first hand. You

14

compare the sports coupe and the minivan by noting that each has the
same sheetmetal, unibody construction, dual airbags, and similar
other safety features. The minivan, however, has considerably more
room for passengers, more storage space, offers optional built-in
child seats, and is generally more versatile than the sports coupe.
Also, the minivan's purchase price is less and it will probably cost
less to maintain over time. In contrasting the two vehicles, you
notice that the coupe definitely has more eye appeal, handles
better, reaches higher speeds faster, and gets better mileage, while
the minivan has a rather basic design, has more of a truck than a
car "feel," and definitely shouts "family transportation!" If you
think that cost and your family's needs should outweigh better
mileage and your desire for a more dashing vehicle, then you will
probably agree to buy the minivan. If, on the other hand, cost
is not a high priority and you think you can squeeze your family
into the coupe for at least a few years, then you will probably
try to convince your spouse to agree to purchase the sports car.

A. THINKING CRITICALLY

In this activity you will compare and contrast the **rights**
and **restrictions** of the elderly and children in American society.
You will base your comments on the following paragraphs which include
excerpts from Sociology, Experiencing Changing Societies (7th ed.)[2]
by Kammeyer, Ritzer and Yetman. You may also use information gathered

---

[2]
Kenneth C. Kammeyer, George Ritzer, and Norman R. Yetman.
Sociology, Experiencing Changing Societies. 7th edition,
Boston: Allyn and Bacon, 1997, pp. 349-353, 355-356.

from other sources (but remember to cite the complete references for these sources).

Age is one ascribed criterion which provides a basis for regulating what certain categories of people can and cannot do in a variety of areas. For example, people _below_ a certain age may NOT quit school, get a job, drive a car, vote, purchase or drink alcohol legally, or get married. While there are probably fewer restrictions based on age as the chronological point _beyond_ _which_ a person may or may not do something, until recently, for example, mandatory retirement laws limited the individual freedom of older workers to choose to work full-time for as long as _they_ wanted and were able.

Every society has "dependent" populations. Traditionally, the dependent population in American society has consisted of children under 15 and adults 65 and older. These are the age categories which generally do not produce income and pay taxes. This fact of life makes them dependent on others in their society who do. The size of the dependent population may vary both across societies and within a society over time.

In 1995, children under 15 comprised about one-fifth of the total United States population whereas those 65 and older contributed about 13% to the total population (Treas 1995). Population projections from the U.S. Census Bureau point to a "graying" of America and increasing life expectancy. By the year 2030, people 65 and older are projected to comprise over 20% of the total population while the percentage of children 15 and under will drop below their 1995 figure.

16

Children in the U.S.

... it is interesting to find that for much of
Western history, childhood was not thought of
as a distinct stage...

Children at a very early age were expected to
participate in productive work...

Today, the situation is quite different, with
children rarely entering the work force until
at least high school age...

Children and adolescents in contemporary American families are usually rather loosely controlled and limited by parents. The assumption
it that their immaturity makes it imprudent to
give them too much freedom...

Some rights that were granted earlier to adolescents and young adults have been withdrawn
in recent years. Many high schools adopted
liberalized policies of dress and behavior in
the 1970s, which have since been retracted.
Smoking, for example, was often allowed in
specified areas of high schools, but in recent years many schools have discontinued this
privilege. In a similar way, many states and
localities in the 1970s lowered the age for
drinking alcoholic beverages to 18. More
recently, the laws have been changed, raising
the legal drinking age in most places to 21...

When age categories are socially defined, certain rights and limitations will be attached
to the people in that category. This system
is referred to as **age stratification.**

The attitude that limitations and restrictions
can be based on age is called **ageism.** Although the term ageism is applied primarily to
the treatment of the elderly, it can generally
refer to any instance when an individual's age
is the primary basis for evaluating and dealing
with that person.

The Elderly in the U. S.

... In the United States it is both the legal
and social custom to use the 65th birthday as the
beginning of old age. When the Social Security
Act was passed in 1935, age 65 was set as the
age when retirement benefits could be received.
Thus, in the public mind, 65 became linked with
old age. However, the laws have changed peri-
odically, and for several decades Americans have
had the option of receiving partial Social Security
benefits at age 62. Beginning in the year 2000,
the age at which full benefits can be received
will increase in gradual steps from age 65 to 67.
Furthermore, as a way of combating age discri-
mination in the occupational world, Congress
passed legislation that allows most workers to
work until age 70, if they wish...

In the contemporary United States, many people
still view age 65 as the beginning of old age,
but new definitions are emerging, particularly
from the older people themselves. Often people
at age 65 and even older do not think of themselves as old because they have a level of health
and a style of life that they do not associate
with old age (Treas 1995)...

The Economic Condition
of the Elderly and Children

Just as the physical lives of many older people
have been improving, so have their economic lives.
There is definitely a bright side to the economic
condition of the elderly population today, but
there is also a dark side...

The high percentages of early retirement among
men today probably reflects the fact that they
are economically able to retire...

Elderly people's incomes come partly from Social
Security, which accounts for about 40 percent of
the total, and a slightly larger percentage comes
from pensions and assets. Older Americans also
received noncash benefits in the form of Medicare
and Medicaid...

... The majority of older people have some economic resources in real estate, savings, and invest-
ments...

... But now we turn to that part of the elderly
population where the economic picture is much
darker.   Some people have reached old age who are
perhaps in poor health and with physical disabil-
ities, who do not own homes, and who have no savings or other assets.   Often, their monthly rent
takes a substantial part of their only money
income-- Social Security benefits.   These elderly
people live in very precarious economic conditions,
often in poor, dilapidated housing...

In 1993, according to the federal government's
poverty standard, 12 percent of the elderly are
living in poverty-- with the old-old having a
higher percentage in poverty than the young-old
(U. S. Bureau of the Census 1995b).   However,
the most serious poverty exists among elderly
women and elderly minorities (Harel et al.
1990, Soldo and Agree 1988).   Elderly women have
a significantly higher level of poverty (15 percent) than elderly men (8 percent).   Elderly
blacks have a much higher poverty level than
elderly whites (31 percent as compared to 11
percent), while elderly Hispanics are at an
intermediate level (22.5 percent).   The most
seriously impoverished are elderly black women
who live alone;   a full 60 percent of these
women are below the poverty level...

Although many elderly in the United States are
poor, even more poverty exists among the children
of the society.   In 1993, 22 percent of all
children under 18 years old were living in house-
holds where incomes were below the poverty level
(U. S. Bureau of the Census 1995b).   Among black
children the percentage was 46 percent;   among
Hispanic children it was 40 percent...

The disturbing trend in the United States is
that, while poverty levels for the elderly have
been going down, the poverty rate for children
has been going up (Hernandez 1995).   Government
expenditures for the elderly have been increasing, while programs for children have been going
down.   The major program for children (Aid to
Families with Dependent Children) has not kept
up with inflation since 1970   (Johnson et al.
1991).   Public and political opposition to welfare in the 1990s threatens even more cuts in
welfare programs for children. (Kammeyer, Ritzer
            and Yetman 1997, pp. 349-353, 355-356)

19

1. List several ways in which the children under 15 and adults over 65 are similar.

_____

_____

_____

_____

_____

2. List several ways in which they different.

_____

_____

_____

_____

3. Do you think these similarities and differences are important? If so, why? If not, why not?

_____

_____

_____

B. **THINKING ABOUT THINKING**

4. In your own words, describe what you thought as you compared and contrasted children and the elderly in questions 1 and 2 of Part A.

_____

_____

_____

_____

5. Sometimes when you compare and contrast things, you may do this hastily and miss important similarities and differences.

    When you buy a new sweater, for example, you may only compare the **prices** of the sweaters you see and not consider how long each will last or how each will look after a few wearings.

    Try to come up with some strategies which you can use to pick out as many important similarities and differences as possible between two items. Describe your strategies.

    _____

    _____

    _____

    _____

C. **APPLYING WHAT YOU HAVE LEARNED**

6. Suppose you are at the point where you must make a choice of a major, job, or graduate school. You have narrowed down the options to two (majors, jobs, or graduate schools) but, to date, you have been unable to decide which of the two alternatives is probably best for you.

    Focus on one of the above life choices (major, new job, or graduate school) and use some comparing and contrasting skills to help you make your decision. If necessary, do some "research" to provide some objective information to assist you in making your decision.

    a. Identify what are you comparing and contrasting:

        _____

    b. Use comparing and contrasting skills to make a decision:

    _____

    _____

    _____

    _____

21

7. Consider an item that you purchased recently (such as an article of clothing, a CD, or a stereo) that is comparable to, but different from, an item purchased by a friend of yours. Why did you decide to buy that item instead of the one your friend bought?

_____

_____

_____

_____

IV. **GENERALIZING**

Whenever you draw a conclusion about an entire **group** (e.g. a college club), **aggregate** (e.g., your sociology class), or **population** (e.g., the population of the college or university you attend) based on information about only SOME rather than ALL members, you are making a generalization. In sociology, most of our generalizations are based on studying samples drawn from (usually large) populations rather than on studying whole populations.

Generalizations are <u>statements of probability</u> (that is, are more or less likely) <u>not certain conclusions</u>. The probability that a generalization is correct increases with the <u>size</u> of the sample studied, the degree to which the sample is <u>representative</u> of the entire group, aggregate, or population, and the <u>accuracy of the information gathered</u> from or about the sample.

Whenever we generalize from a sample characteristic (known as a statistic) to a population characteristic (known as a parameter), there is always the chance of some discrepancy between the two. This discrepancy is known as sampling error.

Suppose, for example, you are interested in finding out the average weekly income of full-time day students who work for pay (part-time vs. full-time) at your college/university. However, since the total population of students is too large to study, you decide to get information a sample of 30 employed students known to you and your friends. You ask around until you come up with the names of 30 students who work. Then you contact each of these students to find out how much s/he earned last week and how many hours each worked. From this information you calculate the **mean**

23

weekly income earned for full- and part-time working students.
Can you generalize <u>legitimately</u> from this statistic to the mean
weekly income of ALL working students at the college? The answer
is **NO**, because your sample is biased. You might think that the
bias is due to the small sample size. Although it is true that
sampling error increases as sample size decreases, in this situation
even a large sample would not offset the limitation resulting from
the way the sample of working students was selected. While it may
seem that you selected your sample "randomly," you actually got the
students in a non-random way. Specifically, you drew what sociologists call an "accidental" or "convenience" sample. Instead of
giving every working student in the day school an equal chance of
being chosen and questioned, you relied on easily available students.
The former describes a random or probability sample-- the type you
must choose if you want to generalize legitimately from sample
statistic to population parameter. When you collect information
from a sample selected in a non-random way, you can only use the
information to describe the sample. Unfortunately, however, generalizations based on information from non-random samples is all
too common. It is this type of ill-founded generalizing or over-
generalizing that often leads to stereotyping.

A. **THINKING CRITICALLY**

In this exercise, you will play the role of a social researcher studying homeless or "street" people in the city where the college or university you attend is located. You and a classmate spend several afternoons at several shelters and soup kitchens in the city, observing the behavior of the street people you see. One thing you notice is that homeless men eat alone and keep to themselves while homeless women seem to sit and eat with other women or with children.

1. Based on your observations, formulate a general statement (generalization) about the affiliation patterns of homeless men and women. Make sure your generalization is not too broad.

   Generalization: _____

   _____

2a. Who is more likely to be friendly to strangers, a homeless male or a female?

   ( ) male   ( ) female

b. Can you draw a conclusion from the evidence presented here? Explain your reasoning.

   ( ) yes   ( ) no

   Explanation: _____

   _____

   _____

B. **THINKING ABOUT THINKING**

3. Describe the thinking process you went through
    in formulating your generalization in question 1.

    _____

    _____

    _____

    _____

4. Explain the thinking you did in reaching a con-
    clusion in question 2.

    _____

    _____

    _____

    _____

5. From your answer to question 4, determine whether
    or not your decision was based on an ill-founded
    generalization.

    _____

    _____

    _____

C. **APPLYING WHAT YOU HAVE LEARNED**

6. You tell a friend that you are going to a concert
    with your music appreciation class. Her response
    is "Yuck! All classical music concerts are boring!"

    What questions would you ask her in order to deter-
    mine whether or not her generalization was well-
    founded?

    _____

    _____

    _____

7a. If you encountered a rattlesnake, why would you
    try to avoid it?

    ( ) yes   ( ) no

b. Is it valid to generalize that all rattlesnakes are
    dangerous? Why or why not?

    ( ) yes   ( ) no

    Explanation: _____

    _____

    _____

8a. Are each of the following statements <u>valid general-
    izations</u>?

    1. "Smoking is hazardous to your health."

        ( ) yes   ( ) no

    Explain your answer: _____

    _____

    2. "Marijuana use is hazardous to your health."

        ( ) yes   ( ) no

    Explain your answer: _____

    _____

    _____

    3. "Cocaine use is hazardous to your health."

        ( ) yes   ( ) no

    Explain your answer: _____

    _____

    _____

b. Are these statements necessarily true OR probably true?

Statement #1: ( ) necessarily true

( ) probably true

Explain: _____

_____

Statement #2: ( ) necessarily true

( ) probably true

Explain: _____

_____

Statement #3: ( ) necessarily true

( ) probably true

Explain: _____

_____

V. READING the POPULAR MEDIA WITH a CRITICAL EYE

The popular media-- newspapers, popular magazines, and television, for example-- are important sources of information as well as entertainment. However, the mass of information to which readers and viewers are exposed is not all of the same quality or even uniformly based on "objective" evidence. So, reading and viewing with a critical eye is an important skill which should be acquired by observers of the social scene, including students, consumers, professionals in a variety of fields, etc.. We would put a lot more confidence in a news story reported in the New York Times than in one reported in a tabloid. Even in a good quality news medium, some articles are hard news, based on well-documented, reputable sources, whereas others are softer reports, lifestyle discussions, point of view or opinion pieces (like those found in an Editorial Section).

A critical reader needs to ask insightful questions about what she or he reads. Such questions would include, for example:

- What "evidence" is presented to support the author's position? How "good" is the evidence? What is its source? From whom was it gathered?

- How much influence do reporters' or writers' personal points of view or biases have on what they write?

- How much influence do editors have on what gets published?

- How might outside forces like powerful lobbists or advertisers affect the orientation/slant, content, or even the chances of inclusion of articles on controversial topics (especially those about issues which clash with, or call into question, products advertised in the magazines such as alcohol or cars).

29

- And what about advertisements? How much confidence should readers or viewers place in the claims they contain?

A. **THINKING CRITICALLY**

In this exercise you will be evaluating the accuracy of an advertising message. Product statements and advertisements are often based on <u>claims of results</u> (e.g., medically proven to regrow hair, guaranteed to lower cholesterol, will reduce weight by at least 10 lbs in 30 days, etc.) or <u>endorser support</u> (e.g., dermatologists conducted 12-month clinical tests..., studies indicate that ..., or "J. D. Powers and Associates has ranked ____ the most appealing full-size sport utility based on owner rankings of over 100 attributes including style, comfort and performance" [<u>Time</u>, July 21, 1997]) which may or may not be what they seem.

Imagine that you have seen a number of advertisements in magazines about a new type of American-built car. Advertisers say the following about it:

> "... The overall size, comfort and convenience of this car, not to mention terrific performance, make it a winner" (<u>Auto Week</u>, February, 1994).

> "It's an American car that can hold its own in any company, on any kind of road" (<u>Automobile Magazine</u>, January, 1993).

> "... exceeds standards set by the best imports in 3 their class" (<u>Worth Magazine</u> October/November, 1992).

3

All of these statements are quoted from <u>U.S. News & World Report</u> (October, 1994).

1. What kinds of questions would you want answered
   in order to decide whether the information in
   the advertisement is reliable or unreliable?

   _____

   _____

   _____

2a. What can you tell from the message that leads
    you to believe that it is either reliable or
    unreliable?

    _____

    _____

    _____

 b. Describe some other things you could find out
    about this information and its source that
    would lead you to think it was either reliable
    or unreliable.

    _____

    _____

3. Can you imagine getting information about this
   car from another source that would be more reliable? less reliable? Describe each source
   and explain why you think it is more or less
   reliable.

   _____

   _____

   _____

   _____

31

B.   **THINKING ABOUT THINKING**

4.   Describe the thinking steps you took in question 2
     to decide whether or not the information presented
     in the message is reliable.

_____

_____

_____

5.   What advice would you give to someone who is
     trying to decide whether or not a piece of
     advertising information is reliable?

_____

_____

C.   **APPLYING WHAT YOU HAVE LEARNED**

6.   Locate an article on a topic of interest to you
     in a popular medium (i.e., a magazine or newspaper).

a.   Using the questions listed in part A 1-3 as a guide,
     evaluate the article as to the quality (i.e., strength,
     logic, and consistency) of the argument made, probable
     reliability of evidence cited or claims made.

Title, Author(s), Source and Date of article, Pages:

_____

_____

Critique: _____

_____

_____

_____

_____

_____

continue ...

_____

_____

_____

_____

_____

b. How might you check on the reliability of the claims or
    conclusions made in this article?

_____

_____

_____

_____

_____

VI. DESCRIBING VERSUS EXPLAINING

In this critical thinking activity, the focus is on the distinction and connection between description and explanation. We will talk about how to do simple causal analyses involving a three-variable model which contains a proposed cause (X), a proposed effect (Y), and one control variable (Z or TF) and how to interpret the outcomes of such analyses by using the Elaboration Model. In the next critical thinking activity-- Activity VII-- the emphasis will be on understanding and using more complex causal models.

Your knowledge of the social world is derived from answering questions about WHAT and WHY. WHAT questions have a descriptive intent whereas WHY questions have a explanatory or causal intent. When you ask about the **characteristics** of some group, organization or population, the **frequency of occurrence** of some behavior or attitude or **whether and in what direction one variable is associated (or correlated) with another,** you are asking descriptive questions. When you observe an association between two variables and ask why they are associated, you are moving from description to explanation.

An association between two variables may vary in strength as well as in direction. The **strength** of an association is generally somewhere between 0 (no association) and +/- 1.00 (a perfect association). Most associations probably fall into the low to moderate range; some could aptly be described as strong. Perfect associations are a rarity in the social world. The **direction** of an association between two quantitative variables which have a linear or

34

straight-line relationship is described as either positive (⟋)
or negative ⟍). In a positive (or direct) association, Y increases (or decreases) for a given unit of increase (or decrease)
in X, such that both change in the same direction, either increasing
or decreasing together. In a negative (indirect or inverse) association, X and Y change in opposite ways: that is, for every unit
of increase in X, there is a given amount of decrease in Y. Some
correlations between variables are curvilinear or u-shaped. An
example of a curvilinear association is that between social class
and family size. Both the lower and the upper classes tend to have
larger numbers of children than does the middle class. So the
shape of such a relationship looks like a U (⌣). A curvilinear association is actually a combination of an indirect and a
direct relationship, depending on which attributes or categories
of the Independent Variable you are examining.

Description lays the foundation for explanation by pointing
out potentially relevant variables to study in a particular area
of interest. However, explanation goes beyond description by
requiring that, in addition to showing that a correlation exists,
a researcher also deal with two other necessary criteria. First,
s/he must show that the proposed cause happened or changed before
the proposed effect. This process is known as establishing time
order. Next, s/he must demonstrate that the correlation between
the variables is not spurious, that is, that it **cannot** be "explained away" as due to a third variable which is the cause of
both X and Y. This third criterion is referred to as eliminating
competing hypotheses. Russell Schutt (1996) adds a fourth criter-

ion to the list: mechanism. Schutt notes that our confidence in finding a true causal connection is strengthened if we can show the mechanism through which the Independent Variable is related to the Dependent Variable. Stated simply, Intervening Variables, described below, operate as causal mechanisms (Schutt 1996, p. 121).

Third variables (also called Test Factors or Control Variables) are of two types: Antecedent or Intervening. If a third variable occurs before both the proposed cause (X) and the proposed effect (Y) in time, it is known as an **Antecedent** Test Factor. Antecedent Variables may operate as the cause of both X and Y. Controlling for such variables, then, allows us to see what happens to the original relationship between X and Y. If we have isolated a true antecedent variable, this relationship should disappear because it was spurious. The time ordering of the third variable may place it between the proposed cause and the proposed effect, thus earning it the label of **Intervening** Test Factor. Intervening Variables are influenced by the Independent Variables and, in turn, influence the Dependent Variable. The causal model for each Test Factor (TF) in relation to X and Y is as follows:

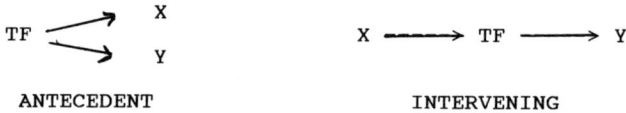

$$TF \overset{\textstyle\longrightarrow}{\underset{\textstyle\longrightarrow}{}} \begin{matrix} X \\ \\ Y \end{matrix} \qquad\qquad X \longrightarrow TF \longrightarrow Y$$

$$\text{ANTECEDENT} \qquad\qquad\qquad \text{INTERVENING}$$

Multi-variate analysis is the basic model for testing causal hypotheses because it allows us to see what happens to the original association between X and Y when the Test Factor is introduced. So, the simplest type of multi-variate analysis involves examining the

36

effects of a <u>single Test Factor</u> on the X - Y relationship. Each
part (or sub-table) of the multi-variate table is called a "partial."
When a test factor is divided into two attributes (for example,
"high" and "low"), a three-variable table contains <u>two</u> partials.
When the Test Factor contains three attributes (for example, high
school graduation or less [0-12 years of schooling], some college
[1 - 3 years of college], and college graduation or beyond [4+
years of college], the three-variable table contains three partials.

It is possible to examine the effects of several Test Factors
on the X-Y relationship simultaneously. The point to remember,
however, is that Test Factors are NOT introduced haphazardly into
any analysis. They are chosen on the basis of logic, theoretical
importance, or because they were previously shown to have empirical
relevance to X and Y.

The process of repeatedly introducing a Test Factor into a
bi-variate (X and Y) relationship is called the "Elaboration Model."[4]
The Elaboration Model or Elaboration Analysis is a process through
which social researchers try to "explain" or "specify" the relationship between X and Y by means of a Test Factor-- thus making
that relationship more meaningful or exact. Elaboration helps us
to answer the questions of "why" and "under what circumstances."
Once we have shown that X and Y are corrrelated and that X happened
or changed before Y, we are ready to use the Elaboration Model.
The Elaboration Model may yield four possible outcomes, illustrated
in the table which follows:

---

[4] This model was developed by sociologist Paul F. Lazarsfeld.

Partial Relationships Compared with Original	"Test Factor"	
	ANTECEDENT	INTERVENING

- Partials same as original ------------> REPLICATION

- Partials less than original
  or approximate zero (no assn.)--> EXPLANATION or INTERPRETATION

- One partial is same or greater
  while other is less or zero (split) --> SPECIFICATION

Let's look how the Elaboration Model works by means of a
familiar example and some hypothetical ("mock") data.   Classroom
dynamics are always of interest to sociology instructors.   One
dynamic of particular is the potential influence of where students
sit on their level of class participation and grade in a course.
Similarly, one wonders what causes some students to choose a seat
in the front of the room on a regular basis while others gravitate
consistently toward the back rows.

Suppose a sociology instructor observes that students who sit
at the front of the classroom in Introductory Sociology are more
likely than those who sit in the back to have high levels of participation in class discussions.   This association, or descriptive
observation, is illustrated through the hypothetical data provided
in Table 1:

-----

[5] For a detailed discussion of the history of the Elaboration Model and how it works, see: Earl R. Babbie, <u>The Practice
of Social Research</u>, 8th Ed. Belmont, CA: Wadsworth Publishing
Co., 1998, Chapter 16.

Table 1. Level of Class Participation by Seating Position
         of Students in Introductory Sociology

Level of Class Participation	Seating Position			
	Rows 1-3		Rows 4-6	
	%	N	%	N
High	67		37	
		(20)		(11)
Low	33		63	
		(10)		(19)
Total	100		100	
		(30)		(30)

Focus on the "High" row in Table 1. Comparing these two cells
shows that 67% of the students who sit in the front of the room
(in rows 1-3) have a high level of class participation as compared
to 37% of those who sit in the back of the room (in rows 4-6). The
% difference is 30% (67% - 37% = 30%). In the absence of a statistical test and for the sake of simplicity, let's assume that a
difference this large is significant (e.g., not likely to be due to
chance).

Is seating position the **cause** of level of class participation? Maybe and maybe not. In order to establish a causal connection between seating position and level of class participation,
the instructor must 1) make a case for the time priority of
seating position and 2) test one (or more) competing hypothesis/
hypotheses. The time priority of seating position over the level
of class participation makes logical sense because students choose
(or are assigned their seats) at the beginning of the semester and,
typically, those seating patterns persist for the whole semester.

39

Class discussions usually take place at various points during the semester after specific material is covered. So far so good.

Now the instructor is ready to introduce a third variable to the table. She chooses degree of interest as her Test Factor and hypothesizes that both seating position and level of class participation may be functions of (or dependent on) interest in the course content. If her hypothesis is valid, then introducing degree of interest should result in a reduction of the size of the association between seating position and level of class participation in each partial. Note the causal model which diagrams the instructor's hypothesis:

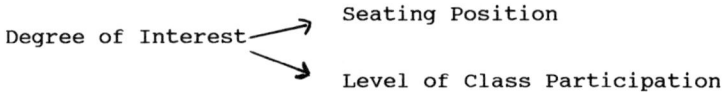

Degree of Interest ➔ Seating Position

➔ Level of Class Participation

In this model, degree of interest plays the role of an Antecedent Variable.

Table 2 shows what happens when degree of interest is introduced as the third or control variable. Focus again on the "high" category of class participation by seating position but do it **within the high and low degree of interest** partials. Calculate the percentage difference for each partial and compare this difference to the one we obtained for Table 1. Based on the hypothetical data in Table 2, what can the instructor conclude about which variable-- seating position or degree of interest-- is the real cause of level of class participation?

Table 2. Degree of Interest, Seating Position, and Level of Class
          Participation of Students in Introductory Sociology

| | HIGH Interest | | | | LOW Interest | | | |
Level of Class Participation	Rows 1-3 %	N	Rows 4-6 %	N	Rows 1-3 %	N	Rows 4-6 %	N
High	67		67		42		33	
		(12)		(8)		(5)		(6)
Low	33		33		58		67	
		(6)		(4)		(7)		(12)
Total	100%	(18)	100%	(12)	100%	(12)	100%	(18)

In partial A (the "High" Interest students), the association between
seating position disappears. In partial B (the "Low" Interest students), the association is greatly reduced (% difference is 9). This
outcome reflects EXPLANATION in the Elaboration Model. The instructor's hypothesis appears to be supported: Interested students tend
to participate at a high level in class discussions-- **regardless
of where they sit.** Among students who have a low degree of interest,
those who sit in front tend to be slightly more active in class discussions than those who sit in back--**but the difference is not
significant.**

When a proposed Independent Variable (X) is a true cause of
the Dependent Variable (Y), no matter how many test factors a
researcher introduces into the X-Y relationship, s/he will always
get the outcome of REPLICATION. Replication means that the original association between X and Y holds up or remains about as
strong as in the original (two-variable) table. Notice that in
Replication the ordering of the Test Factor does not matter.

41

Ordering is also not relevant in SPECIFICATION. If partial B in Table 2 showed a stronger association than it did (e.g., was 10 or greater), then we would have SPECIFICATION rather than EXPLANATION. The sociology instructor would have "specified" a condition under which seating position does affect level of class participation (only among the "less" interested). INTERPRETATION produces the same outcome as EXPLANATION. The only difference is the ordering of the Test Factor which is Intervening rather than Antecedent.

A. **THINKING CRITICALLY**

This part of the exercise gets you to think critically about homeless people, what they are like and how they became homeless.

1. What do you know about homeless people? If you do not know much about them, read one or two articles to give you some background information.

   a. Identify FOUR characteristics of homeless people?

      1. _____

      2. _____

      3. _____

      4. _____

2. LIST **at least FIVE possible causes of homelessness** in American society. Organize these causes under the following headings:

   Social: _____

   _____

   Economic: _____

   _____

Psychological: _____

_____

3. Which **THREE** of these five causes appear to
   be most important?

   a. _____

   b. _____

   c. _____

4. What kind of evidence would tend to rule out
   certain of these causes?

   _____

   _____

   _____

   _____

B. **THINKING ABOUT THINKING**

   5. How did you decide what to list as possible
      explanations for homelessness?

      _____

      _____

      _____

      _____

   6. Describe the sequence of your thinking as you
      attempted to explain WHY homelessness exists
      in American society.

      _____

      _____

      _____

      _____

C. **APPLYING WHAT YOU HAVE LEARNED**

    7.   Develop a causal hypothesis relating one of the variables you listed in question 2 to "the likelihood of becoming homeless" (the Dependent Variable).

    _____

    _____

    _____

    8a.   Identify a third variable (Test Factor or Z) which you think may explain away the relationship between X and Y.

        _____

    b.   Is the third variable you identified above

        ( ) Antecedent   OR   ( ) Intervening?

    9.   Diagram a simple causal model which shows how all three variables are related:

VII. GRASPING the COMPLEXITY of CAUSAL RELATIONSHIPS

Many people think simplistically about cause and effect relationships. For example, they may view one variable (the Independent or X Variable) as having a solo, direct, possibly all-encom-
passing effect on the Dependent or (Y) variable. That is, they
assume that the Independent Variable explains all or a very high
percentage of the change in the Dependent Variable. They may
also focus their investigation on only one small portion of the
causal chain and fail to realize that variables which play the
role of Independent in any given relationship-- particularly
variables like attitudes, behavior, and opportunities-- may themselves have been affected by the operation of one or more other
variables.

Social reality is far more complex than a simplistic "one
cause ———> one effect model" suggests. In fact, what goes on in
the social world reflects the workings of many variables or causes
on one or more outcomes or effects. Likewise, the role played by
any given variable (i.e., cause or effect) depends on where in
the causal sequence we look.

So, in our efforts to grasp cause and effect relationships,
we need to advance from simplistic thinking to a more accurate
understanding of the complexity of such relationships-- from uni-
to multi-causal models and from direct to both direct and indirect
effects.

45

In their search for cause and effect relationships, researchers may use one of two models: idiographic or nomothetic. The **idiographic model** requires that the researcher look for (and test) <u>all</u> of the possible causes of a given outcome. This model or approach tends to be used most commonly in a case studies or, for example, to analyze all of the factors which led up to a given individual's decision to do something (i.e., to choose a particular college, or a particular job). Since the idiographic model tends to be very time-consuming, most social researchers use the nomothetic model which includes only the most important variables explaining a given outcome. The variables so identified would provide a partial but powerful explanation of some phenomenon such as, for example, voting behavior in a national election. The nomothetic approach tends to be used most commonly for analyses of aggregated data like those collected in surveys of large samples.

The goal of sociology and the other social sciences is to explain as much as possible by using as few variables as possible. Therefore, although they usually make a thorough search of the relevant literature on a topic to uncover all possible variables of interest, in their research sociologists generally choose to focus on only the most important (or significant) of the relationships among variables.

For example, if a sociologist is trying to understand what caused a person's social class status (i.e., his/her location in the stratification system of society) and what consequences follow from this position, s/he would attempt to diagram a proposed causal model. The broad strokes of a complex causal model explaining

46

one's location in the stratification system and its consequences
might look like the following:

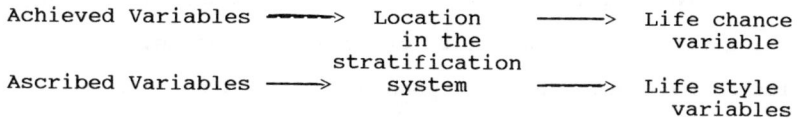

```
Achieved Variables ------>  Location      ------>  Life chance
                            in the                 variable
                         stratification
Ascribed Variables ----->    system      ------>  Life style
                                                  variables
```

This model says that a person's location in the stratification
system is **dependent** on (or caused by) factors over which s/he
has at least some control and has attained, or will attain, through
his/her own efforts and those over which s/he has little or no control. The former would be included under the heading of "achieved"
and the latter under the heading "ascribed. In turn, one's location in the stratification system plays the role of Independent
Variable when it **influences** the life style one enjoys and, more
importantly, the life chances to which one has access. Life style
refers to relatively distinct attitudes, values, and behavior of
people in different social class positions whereas life chances
refer to the likelihood of attaining the "good things in life."

What remains to be identified are the particular variables
which fit into each category-- achieved, ascribed, life style,
and life chance variables, the relative importance of each in influencing a given outcome, and any indirect or interactive effects.
Examples of achieved variables which come to mind include a will-
ingness to work hard, efforts to defer gratification, and saving
and investing one's money. Important ascribed variables include
one's parents' social class position, one's race, gender, age,
family or personal connections or lack of them, good or bad luck,

the nature of the job market, and other macro social conditions. In the category of life style variables sociologists include child-rearing practices, sex-role expectations of husbands and wives, political attitudes and behavior, civic participation, and lei-sure-time activities. The life chance variables a sociologist might investigate would probably include length of life, physical and mental health and access to health care, the amount and quality of the education one receives, and treatment by the law.

The causal sequence which is developed must reflect that some factors have a direct effect whereas others exert their effects indirectly. For example, one's parents' social class position has a direct effect on their offspring's initial social class position. However, another variable, age, may exert it influence indirectly through the operation of the variable of educational level attained.

A. **THINKING CRITICALLY**

In this part of the exercise, you will use a critical thinking approach to examine the complexity of causal relationships. You want to under the most important influences on academic achievement in college.

1. Identify at least five variables which you think are the **most important factors** which influence academic achievement at college. List these variables in order of importance with Variable A being the most important, Variable B, the next most important, and so on.

a. _____ = Variable A

b. _____ = Variable B

c. _____ = Variable C

d. _____ = Variable D

e. _____ = Variable E

2. Set up a causal model showing how each of the
    factors you identified above influence academic
    achievement (the dependent variable). Be sure
    to show both direct and indirect effects on your
    diagram.

                                        Academic
                                        Achievement
                                           (Y)

3. Is your model nomothetic or idiographic?

    ( ) nomothetic ( ) idiographic

    Explain briefly. _____

    _____

    _____

    _____

B. **THINKING ABOUT THINKING**

    4.   How did you decide that the five variables you listed in question 1 are the most important influences on academic achievement?

_____

_____

_____

_____

    5.   If you were not limited to choosing the five most important influences on academic achievement, how many variables would you have come up with?

N = _____

Identify other variables you thin should be considered:

_____

_____

_____

C. **APPLYING WHAT YOU HAVE LEARNED**

    6.   Select two situations (or outcomes) from your life in which you analyze why something happened.

    a.   Briefly identify each situation below.

Situation 1:_____

_____

Situation 2:_____

_____

    b.   Use the **idiographic** causal modeling approach to identify the paths of the relevant causes to the proposed outcome (effect). First list the explanatory variables in your causal model. Use as many spaces as are relevant.

Situation 1: _____   _____

_____   _____

_____   _____

_____   _____

Situation 2: _____   _____

_____   _____

_____   _____

_____   _____

    2.   Diagram your idiographic causal models below. Be
        sure to put your dependent variable on the far
        right and to show both direct and indirect effects.

Situation 1 Model:

Situation 2 Model:

    7.   How would you go about determining whether or not your
        explanatory models are correct?   Refer specifically to
        the Elaboration Model discussed in Exercise VI.

_____

_____

_____

_____

VIII. **PREDICTING PROBABLE OUTCOMES**

When you predict consequences, you draw a conclusion, based
on evidence, about the probable effects of an event. A prediction
is not certain, but it is more likely than a guess because it is
based on sound reasoning from evidence. The probability that a
prediction is correct increases with the **quality** and the **amount**
of supporting evidence.

Suppose that an important basketball game is to be played
this evening between your school and a nearby college. You and
your friends are trying to predict which team will win the game.
You compare the teams' current records-- your team has won three
games and lost three games while the other team has won five games
and lost only one. One friend mentions that the two best players
on your team are injured and will not play in this evening's game.
Another friend points out that the game will be played at the other
college, giving them the "home court" advantage. You and your
friends agree that you do not have any other pertinent evidence that
will help in predicting the winner. So, based on the evidence you
have, you predict that the other team will win the game. Of course,
your prediction may not be borne out, but the evidence does point
to the probability of a win by the other team.

Sociologists are concerned with **patterned** behavior, inter-
actions that are recurrent or repetitive rather than unique. They
assume that people behave in **fairly predictable ways**. If this
assumption is true, then valid descriptions and explanations of behavior patterns should allow us to predict likely behavior or outcomes in given situations.

Predictions, in turn, can provide a basis for changing or controlling various aspects of the social environment. For example, if variable X (e.g., smoking cigarettes) is a principal cause of variable Y (e.g.,lung cancer), then changing variable X should produce some noticeable changes in variable Y.

When sociologists make predictions, they typically do not focus on the individual level. Rather, in order to increase the likelihood that their predictions will "hold" or be accurate, they focus on the group level (e.g., on families, organizations, communities, societies, etc.), on aggregates, or on whole categories of people (e.g., men as compared with women, people under 30 as compared to those 30 and older, church goers as compared to non-church goers, etc).

A. THINKING CRITICALLY

In this part of the exercise, you will focus on trying to make accurate predictions about the likely effects of increasing the legal drinking age from 18 to 21 on the drinking behavior of adolescents (i.e., those under 21). Since this is a real issue which you may have encountered personally and about which you probably have an opinion, try to 1) recognize any biases you may have and 2) be as objective as possible in making your predictions.

53

1. Make <u>at least two specific predictions</u> about
    the effects of this change in the law on the
    drinking behavior of 18-20 year olds-- who
    formerly were able to buy liquor in package
    stores and bars when the legal drinking age
    in some states was 18, but who are no longer
    able to do so legally now. In formulating
    your predictions, distinguish between those
    who may drink varying amounts-- little or
    none, a moderate amount, a lot (heavy
    drinkers).

Prediction #1: _____

_____

Prediction #2: _____

_____

2. How would you go about determining the accuracy of
    your predictions?

_____

_____

_____

_____

3. How confident would you be in your predictions?

    Before you answer, consider the following situ-
    ation: Suppose a friend who attends college in
    a nearby state invites you to visit for the weekend.
    He tells you that on Saturday night a bunch of his
    friends (ages 19 and 20) are having an off-campus
    party and it's o.k. for you to go along. After
    spending about an hour at the party, your friend
    decides to leave. You are having such a good time,
    however, that you decide to stay longer. Before
    your friend leaves, he tells you to get a ride
    back to his dorm with someone at the party. You
    have made it a rule not to drive with anyone who
    has been drinking.

54

Would you base a decision about whether or not to ask a "typical" party goer for a ride or call a taxi on your predictions (in question 1)?

( ) yes   ( ) no

Explain your reasoning: _____

_____

_____

B. **Thinking About Thinking**

4.   Describe the thinking process that you went through in trying to answer questions 1 and 2.

_____

_____

_____

5.   What advice could you give to a friend who is trying to predict a particular outcome? How would you convince your friend not just to guess?

_____

_____

_____

C. **Applying What You Have Learned**

In this part of the exercise you will be making predictions about the combination of characteristics shared by people who are most and least likely to think that they sometimes drink "too much."[6]

_____

[6]
This exercise was inspired by Exercises #12 (Who Drinks Too Much?) and #13 (Predicting Who Drinks Too Much) developed by Cornelius Riordan and Allan Mazur, Introductory Sociology Workbook (With CHIP Software). New York: Harper and Row, 1988, pp. 87-94.

6. Look over the following list of possible predictor variables and their attributes:

age (younger versus older)

race (white versus non-white)

sex (male versus female)

marital status (married versus single or widowed)

level of happiness (more happy versus less happy)

church attendance (frequent versus infrequent or non-attenders)

level of education (less educated versus more educated)

work status (employed full-time versus employed part-time or unemployed)

occupational prestige (works in high versus low prestige occupations)

a. Based on this list of variables, <u>who</u> do you think tends to drink "too much?" That is, which variable in the list do you think is the probably the **single best predictor** of drinking behavior?

_____

Explain your rationale: _____

_____

_____

b. Which THREE variables on the list do you think would be the BEST predictors of who drinks too much?

_____

_____

_____

EXPLAIN your reasoning: _____

_____

_____

c. What combination of attributes (of the three
    variables you chose in part 6b) best predicts
    who is **most likely** to drink "too much?"

    _____

d. Which of the variables in the list do you think
    would NOT be good predictors of drinking behavior?

    _____

    EXPLAIN: _____

    _____

    _____

7. How would you obtain the data necessary to test the
    accuracy of your predictions? Would you need to
    collect your own data or are there any existing data
    bases which would enable you to test the validity of
    your predictions? BE SPECIFIC.

    _____

    _____

    _____

    _____

8. Identify two social variables (not on the list) which
    you think would be good predictors of drinking behavior.

    _____

    _____

57

IX. COLLECTING FIRST-HAND OBSERVATIONS and EVALUATING THEIR RELIABILITY

There are really only two ways to gather primary social data: you can ask people questions or you can observe their behavior, either from the perspective of a participant in the interaction or as a non-participant. You can, of course, combine asking and observing in the same study. This exercise will focus on helping you to sharpen your ability to evaluate the reliability of an observer and the accuracy of data gathered by firsthand observation.

Accurate observations gathered by reliable observers are crucial in social science. These observations provide the basic data needed to advance social scientific claims-- from complex explanations about, for example, why some people engage in breaking society's rules on a regular basis while others basically conform to them to predictions about future societal trends.

The accuracy of the data gathered by observation depends on a variety of factors which influence what is noticed or not noticed about an event or social situation. These factors include:

- how experienced, skillful, and unbiased the observer is.

- the quality of the instruments he or she uses, including one's own senses and particular recording devices (i.e., audio or video recorders, detailed checklists, etc.).

- the conceptual orientation used to "frame" the observation situation, based on training and past experience.

- the number and quality of the observers used.

Errors may occur when the observer's sight or hearing are impaired, when s/he over-interprets what is being observed, when s/he uses inadequate recording devices, or too few or biased observers. So, firsthand observation can be quite accurate or quite inaccurate.

Students interested in studying human behavior need to be aware of the factors that may influence the accuracy of observations-- one's own as well as those collected by others. Suppose, for example, a sociology instructor asks her students to gather data on informal interaction patterns among students in the college cafeteria during a specified time of the day within a week. The instructor reviews the basics of what to observe and record and the importance of separating one's observations from interpretation (i.e., deciding what the observations mean) with her students in class on the day before the observations are to begin.

Below is a description of how each of four students approach this assignment:

- Paul is uncertain about what to observe because he was absent from the class discussion about the technique.

- Chris knew what she was supposed to look for and record but she was distracted several times when her friends stopped by her table to chat.

- Alex observed and recorded only the behavior of the best-looking students.

- Sue attended the class, knew what behaviors to look for, focused her attention on a section of the cafeteria which was manageable for one person to observe, prepared a detailed checklist (to fill in the who, what, when, where, and why), recorded what she observed while the behavior was taking place, and separated her observations from her interpretations.

Answer the following questions before you read further:

> If you were asked to judge the probable reliability
> of each of these students and the accuracy of their
> observations, who would you choose as the most
> reliable observer?

———————————————————

> Why are that student's observations likely to be the
> most accurate?

———

———

Hopefully, Sue was your choice. She was the most reliable observer

and her observations were the most accurate because she was alert,

well prepared-- had the knowledge about how and what to observe--

and made good use both of her senses and a standardized recording

device (i.e., her checklist).

When there is a chance of error in someone's observations, you

may need to use some other method in order to check for reliability.

In such cases, you may want to look for other evidence that supports

or strengthens what the observer has reported; you may also want to

check out the observer's credentials and whether s/he stands to gain

or lose something important by the way the data are interpreted.

A. **THINKING CRITICALLY**

In this exercise, you will judge the reliability of a person's

observations about the drinking patterns of students at an off-

campus party. Suppose the observer tells you that about 50 people

attended this party over the three-hour period that the observer

was present. The observer also tells you that most of the students

in attendance were drinking beer but that more females than males

60

got drunk. The music was so loud it could be heard a block away. A fight broke out between three or four males at which point the neighbors called the police and the observer left.

1a. What would you try to find out about the observer and his or her observations that would help you decide whether or not to accept the observations and interpretation as accurate and the observer as reliable?

About the Observer   About the Observations

_____

_____

_____

b. Make a list of questions that you would want to have answered before you believed that the observations were accurate.

_____

_____

_____

_____

2. In seeking answers to your list of questions, what might you find out that would count in favor of the observer's reliability? What might you find out that would count against his or her reliability? Make a list of pros and cons.

Pro Observer Reliability   Con Observer Reliability

_____

_____

_____

_____

_____

3. Suppose you could not get answers to many of your questions about the observer, what else might you do to help determine the credibility of the observations?

_____

_____

_____

B. **THINKING ABOUT THINKING**

4. Describe the thinking steps you took to produce your list of questions in answer to question 1.

_____

_____

_____

_____

5. What advice could you give to help other students

a. make judgments about the accuracy of observations made by others

_____

_____

_____

b. make their own observations as accurate as possible.

_____

_____

_____

C.   **APPLYING WHAT YOU HAVE LEARNED**

   6.   Suppose there is an automobile accident in
        which two cars collide. The following people
        witness the accident:

        ● A person getting into a taxi on the
          other side of the street

        ● A person in the third-floor apartment
          of a building on the same street as the
          accident

        ● A police officer directing traffic
          at an intersection a block away

        ● A three-year-old passenger in the back
          seat of one of the cars that collided

        ● The driver of one of the cars that
          collided

        ● A pedestrian who was walking nearby
          when the accident occurred

        ● a business person coming out of a
          bar after happy hour.

        Which of the above witnesses would you consider
        the

   a.   **most reliable?** _____

        Explain: _____

        _____

   b.   **least reliable?**

        Explain: _____

        _____

7. What might you ask the people described in
    question 6 in order to make a better judgment
    of their reliability as witnesses?

    _____

    _____

    _____

    _____

8. Suppose you were interested in gathering in-
    formation about interaction and friendship
    patterns among the college students who live
    on a particular floor of a large college
    dormitory. You want to find out who appears
    to be friendly with whom, who is most popular,
    least popular, where interaction [like social-
    izing and studying] tends to take place, etc.).

    What steps would you take to make sure you get
    accurate observational reports? Briefly dis-
    cuss whom you would bring along to observe
    with you, how you would conduct the observa-
    tions, and what kind of recording device or
    equipment you would use.

    _____

    _____

    _____

    _____

    _____

    _____

X. EVALUATING INFORMATION GATHERED or REPORTED By OTHERS: THE EMPIRICAL RESEARCH ARTICLE/REPORT

Imagine the amount of time you would have to spend if all the knowledge you acquired had to come from your own firsthand observations or through questioning others. Fortunately, you can learn a lot about the workings of the social world and about the behavior of individuals and groups from articles and reports written by others based on information they have gathered or obtained.

The **data** reported in an empirical article may be primary data or secondary data. Primary data are observations collected by the researcher who has written the research report. If a researcher obtains or acquires data from another source-- for example, from another researcher or from a data center-- and uses those data to answer a different research question or to test a new hypothesis, these are called secondary data and s/he is engaged in **secondary analysis**. A good example of secondary analysis is using data from the General Social Survey (GSS) to answer new research questions or to test new hypotheses.

Articles, reports, and books written by others are described as **secondary** sources. So, when you read a journal article or your sociology textbook, you are being exposed to a secondary or secondhand source of information. If the authors of an article did not collect the information they report on themselves but, rather, report on information collected by a third party, we call this a third-hand or **tertiary** source. These distinctions may seem to be confusing. But they are useful in helping you to recognize your proximity or distance from the original source of the data.

So, in sum, primary data/source = you (or a person) observing or
asking; secondary data/source = you (a person) obtaining, re-
analyzing, and reporting on data originally collected by someone
else; tertiary/data source = you reporting/citing information/
data which you neither collected yourself nor obtained from
someone else (who collected it himself) but rather read about the
results of someone's else's (a third party's) secondary analysis
report.

Whenever you read about information gathered or reported
by others, it is important to determine the reliability of the source
and the validity of the information offered. Judging the reliability
of a source means making a decision about how much confidence you can
place in the person who, or organization which, produced the data and
the article. Judging the reliability of a source is more important
when you are reading material in the "popular" media than in the
"scholarly" or professional media, although the issue of reliability
should merit consideration in both. In empirical reports, the term
reliability refers to the consistency of results over time when the
same measure is used to observe relatively enduring characteristics
like age, social class, I. Q., and attitudes toward various issues,
for example.

In essence, evaluating the validity of the data reported in an
empirical article involves determining whether the data answer the
question the author posed sufficiently well (internal validity) and
whether the results (based on the data) can be extended or gener-
alized beyond the sample studied to some population or to a different context (external validity). So, in regard to an empirical

66

or data-based article which has been accepted for publication in a professional journal, your major concern should be with the validity of the results-- both internal and external. That is, has the researcher done an adequate job, for example, in establishing a causal relationship among the variables examined in relation to his/her research purpose (internal validity)? Has s/he made a convincing argument for the generalizability of the results.

Research reports which appear in social science journals usually contain the following components:

1. An Abstract: A brief summary of the important features and results of the research.

2. Introduction: A paragraph or two which places the study in the context of relevant research already done in the area; identifies the author's research question and/or purpose [exploration, description or explanation], gives some rationale for why the study is worth doing, and presents one or more hypotheses to be tested.

3. Methods Section: Describes the theoretical and operational definitions of key variables to be studied and, in causal studies, identifies the independent and dependent variables; discusses the design of the study (who/what was studied, how, at what point/points in time, setting of the study) and the sample selection (plan, method, size).

4. Results: Presents the data generally through simple and complex tables and/or graphs which summarize the data or display trends; identifies statistical techniques used and whether or not the hypotheses are supported.

5. Conclusions/Discussion
      Section: Provides a critical appraisal of the
                            results and their implications; may
                            identify strengths and weaknesses of
                            the study and make suggestions for
                            relevant future research.

6. Implications/Applications
      Section: If present, this section draws out
                            the practical relevance of the findings;
                            in causal or explanatory studies, the
                            author may also make predictions about
                            changes in the dependent variable (e.g.,
                            some dysfunctional or problematic be-
                            havior) based on changes or interven-
                            tions in an independent variable (e.g.,
                            participation in some treatment program).

6. References: A list of all sources cited in the liter-
                            ature review or elsewhere in the report.

A.   **THINKING CRITICALLY**

      In this part of the exercise you will think critically about

information gathered ore reported in the published sociological

literature.

      1.   Find THREE examples of empirical (data-based)
           reports published in one or more sociology
           journals-- for example, in Social Problems,
           The Journal of Social Issues, or Social
           Forces.

           For each of the articles, you will identify the
           data reported in each of the articles as primary
           or secondary. At least one of the articles you
           select must be based on secondary data. Be
           sure to cite the complete reference for each
           article.

      a.   Article #1:

           Author(s): _____

           Title: _____

                      _____

           Journal: _____

68

Volume and Date/Year: _____

Pages: _____

This article is based on:

    ( ) primary data   ( ) secondary data

EXPLAIN: _____

_____

_____

Article #2:

Author(s): _____

Title: _____

          _____

Journal: _____

Volume and Date/Year: _____

Pages: _____

This article is based on:

    ( ) primary data   ( ) secondary data

EXPLAIN: _____

_____

_____

Article #3:

Author(s): _____

Title: _____

          _____

Journal: _____

Volume and Date/Year: _____

Pages: _____

This article is based on :

      ( ) primary data   ( ) secondary data

EXPLAIN: _____

_____

_____

2. Briefly evaluate the **reliability** and **validity** of the information gathered in each article.

<u>Article #1:</u>   <u>Article #2:</u>   <u>Article #3:</u>

Validity: _____

_____

_____

_____

Reliability: _____

_____

_____

_____

B. **THINKING ABOUT THINKING**

3. Describe the thinking steps you took in question 2.

_____

_____

_____

4. What advice would you give to someone who is trying to decide whether or not an empirical report is valid and reliable?

_____

_____

_____

C. **APPLYING WHAT YOU HAVE LEARNED**

5. Select ONE of the data-based research reports you located for question 1 OR an article assigned by your instructor and use the evaluation steps which follow as a guide to your critical review of the article.

   Provide the complete citation for the article you are critically evaluating:

   _____

   _____

   a. <u>Identify your overall purpose in reading the article</u>. (e.g., to discover basic information or to use/apply the results in some way.)

      ( ) basic   ( ) applied

   b. <u>Get an overview of the article</u> by skimming the title, Abstract, Conclusion/Discussion, and, if present, the Application/Implications section. In a few sentences, summarize what the article is about.

      _____

      _____

      _____

      _____

71

c. Identify any biases you may have (for or against) and knowledge of the topic, method(s) used, and analysis.

_____

_____

_____

d. <u>Read the article more carefully. Assess its strengths and weaknesses</u>. You especially want to consider both the thoroughness and the timeliness (how up-to-date) of the literature review; any serious flaws in the way the study was designed, how the data were obtained or gathered, how the sample was selected (random or non-random,) its size, and how the results interpreted. Do the data support the author's conclusions? If you have some basic knowledge of the statistics tests or techniques used, do they appear to be appropriate for these data?

<u>Strengths</u>: _____

_____

_____

<u>Weaknesses</u>: _____

_____

_____

e. <u>Summarize your evaluation</u>. Pull together your thoughts about the article's strengths and weaknesses into a final statement. Assign a score to the article by rating it on a scale from 1 (low) to 10 (high). Justify your rating.

Overall Rating: _____

Evaluation Summary: _____

_____

_____

continue ...

72

_____

_____

_____

_____

_____

_____

f. Do the results have any practical relevance?
    Think carefully about this because the practical
    relevance of the findings may not be stated.

    ( ) yes   ( ) no

EXPLAIN: _____

_____

_____

g. What you can learn about the author's credentials
    and expertise pertinent to the research topic
    investigated? About his/her reliability as a
    second-hand source? If there is no information
    about the author in the journal, where else can
    you look to help you answer this question?

_____

_____

_____

_____

6. How might you confirm your evaluation?.

_____

_____

_____

_____

XI. **MAKING DECISIONS**

You make decisions every day. Many of these are "small"--
i.e., what to wear or what to have for dinner; but some are "big"--
i.e., the choice of a college major or a post-college job. Good
thinking skills can play an important role in helping you to examine alternatives rationally. And, this assessment process should
increase the likelihood that you will make the most informed decision possible.

It is important to learn how to make sound decisions because
these decisions can have implications or future consequences-- some
of which may be far-reaching. For example, on a personal level,
the academic credentials a person has achieved (or the lack of
them) influence the type, level, and salary of his/her first full-
time job. In turn, the type of work experience that person has
accumulated affects the kinds of future jobs she or he is likely
to get.

Value judgements are also involved in the decisions we make--
either explicitly or implicitly. So, ultimately our decisions reflect varying combinations of rational thought and what we think
is "good" or "right" for us to do in a particular set of circumstances.

A. **THINKING CRITICALLY**

In this exercise, you will focus on making the series of decisions involved in narrowing down a suitable topic for a research
paper for sociology course. Suppose your instructor tells you that
you must write an eight page paper on either date or acquaintance

74

Topic #2: _____

_____

_____

_____

_____

7. Based on your answers to question 6, which topic would you choose?

   ( ) Topic #1   ( ) Topic #2

8a. Given the factors that you are sure about and those that are as yet unknown, how confident are you of your choice?

   ( ) very confident ( ) pretty confident

   ( ) not very confident

   Why? _____

   _____

   b. Is there anything you might find out that would cause you to change your mind?

   ( ) yes   ( ) no

   EXPLAIN: _____

   _____

   _____

B. **THINKING ABOUT THINKING**

9. As you make the decision about the best topic/ thesis to choose for your paper, <u>when</u> do you find it helpful to predict probable outcomes?

Topic #1: _____

_____

Topic #2: _____

_____

10. Why did you choose that specific topic/thesis?
    that is, what are your objectives?

    _____

    _____

11. What research options are available to study
    the topic you chose-- first-hand observation?
    surveys? etc.   .

    _____

    _____

12. What are the consequences of each option?

    First-Hand Observation: _____

    _____

    Surveys: _____

    _____

    Other: _____

    _____

13. What general decision-making plan would you
    recommend to others to help them make decisions
    in a more thorough and thoughtful way?

    _____

    _____

    _____

C. **APPLYING WHAT YOUR HAVE LEARNED**

14a. As an undergraduate student, you have the oppor-
      tunity to select elective courses. If you have
      already chosen one or more elective courses,
      think about your choices. Why did you decide
      on this (these) elective(s)?

      _____

      _____

b. Focusing on the <u>last</u> elective you took, was
    it a good choice? Why?

    (   ) yes   (   ) no

    EXPLAIN: _____

    _____

c. If you have not selected an elective yet, list
    the steps you would take in making a decision
    about which elective to choose.

    _____

    _____

    _____

d. Model the steps on the way you thought about
    selecting the topic for your research paper.

    _____

    _____

    _____

e. Whatever you decided, explain the reasons
    for your choice.

    _____

    _____

    _____

XII. **USING SOCIOLOGY: DRAWING OUT THE IMPLICATIONS FOR CHANGE/APPLICATIONS of THEORY and of RESEARCH RESULTS**

On a common sense level, many people-- including a sizeable number of students-- think of theory and research results and their relationship in inaccurate ways. Common sense notions about theory and facts include the following:

- Theory is viewed as speculation-- mere guesswork-- or as abstract, irrelevant ideas developed by someone in an "ivory tower" located at some distance from the "real world."

- Theory is the concern of philosophers whereas facts are the concern of scientists.

- Theory and facts are viewed as direct opposites.

- Facts are considered to be definite, unquestionable, and self evident.

- Research may be viewed as producing these self evident observations or facts disconnected from a theoretical foundation.

- In regard to the relationship between the two, some people think that, once they are tested and supported, theories cease to exists as theories and become facts.

Actually, sociologists' views of theory and research (or facts) are very different from these common sense notions. For example, sociologists view theories as:

- explanations for facts

- of central concern to scientists across disciplines.

- linked to facts in important ways.

- as remaining at the level of theory even when they are supported by facts.

80

To sociologists, social theories are not just interesting; they

are also practical or useful because they enable us to

- better understand human social behavior and
  events (e.g., cause and effect relationships),

- make predictions about probable future behavior
  and events, and

- suggest where interventions strategies or change
  efforts can be directed-- especially when the
  theories contain or deal with manipulable
  variables like attitudes and behavior.

Theories consist of a set of interrelated propositions about the

nature or patterning of events. The objective of any theory is

to _explain_ events or behavior. When a theory is supported by

the results of many research studies, our confidence in its valid-

ity is increased. Facts need to be described (e.g., examined for

patterns) and explained; they do not speak for themselves. Both

theories and the results of accumulated research (i. e., facts) may

have practical implications which can be useful in informing social

policies on the macro level or for suggesting smaller-scale inter-

ventions/changes on the micro level. Moreover, theories and empirical

research are linked in important ways. Almost five decades ago,

Robert Merton (1968) discussed this connection in a pair of classic

essays in his book, _Social Theory and Social Structure_, first

published in 1949.[7] Besides their obvious connection-- e.g., that

theory points us in the direction of the facts we need to gather to

---

[7]
    Robert K. Merton. _Social Theory and Social Structure_.
Expanded Edition. New York: The Free Press, 1968, Essay #3: "The
Bearing of Sociological Theory on Empirical Research, pp. 139-155
and #4: "The Bearing of Empirical Research on Social Theory",
pp. 156-171.

test it and the facts we gather support, modify, or refute it--
Merton also pointed out a number of other functions which research
has for theory, including

- giving rise to a new theory to explain facts
  which existing theories cannot explain,

- recasting or extending an existing theory,

- refocusing an area of interest through the in-
  vention of a new technique for researching it,

- and clarifying concepts.

Consider, for example, the practical relevance of labeling
theory or of the self-fulfilling prophecy idea. Labeling theory
suggests that labels-- i.e., cheater, liar, homosexual, etc.--
tend to be assigned to people when they engage in visible behavior
or when they have some characteristic, regarded by the larger
society as important, and which sets them apart from others.
Although this theory focuses on behavior which is non-conforming
or deviant from the perspective of the larger society, the label
assigned could be either a deviant one (e.g., drug user) or a
conforming one (e.g., honor student). Once assigned, people so
labeled tend to act in accordance with the label. The implications of this theory for future deviance, then, are that people
labeled as deviant may continue to behave in deviant ways and may
seek out others who both behave similarly and who provide support
for their deviant lifestyle. Based on labeling theory, efforts
to change deviant behavior would most likely focus both on changing the label of deviant and on removing the social supports
for deviance in that person's life (e.g., contact with other deviant

82

individuals). Social supports and role models for conforming

behavior would also have to be put in place.

Like labels, the self-fulfilling prophecy can be a power-

ful force which influences behavior. As Merton (1968) pointed

out, the self-fulfilling prophecy is initially a false definition

of the situation which becomes true when people act on the false

definition. Merton gave the example of a run on a solvent bank.

While the bank may be in good financial shape initially, the

rumor that the bank is in trouble may cause many people to with-

draw their money simultaneously, thus causing the bank to fail.

In a well-known book, Rosenthal and Jacobson (1989) reported on

the results of their test of the self-fulfilling prophecy in an

elementary school classroom.[8] These researchers discovered that

suggesting a false belief to teachers-- that 20% of the students

in their classes would spurt academically-- resulted in the belief

coming true. Teachers apparently paid more attention to the chil-

dren whom they expected to "bloom" intellectually (the Experimental

Group) than they did to those whom they did not expect to bloom

(the Control Group), resulting in the former gaining more points

than the latter on a criterion measure of IQ. The most dramatic

differences were reported among the first and second graders.

Although, a follow-up test two years later showed that the "early

bloomers" in the earlier grades lost their initial advantage where-

as those in the upper grades increased theirs, this study leaves

little doubt that the self-fulfilling prophecy idea actually works.

------

[8]
     Robert Rosenthal and Lenore Jacobson. Pygmalian in the
Classroom. New York: Irvington Publishers, 1989.

And, as with labeling, the outcome may be positive or negative, depending on what the belief which defines the situation.

A. **THINKING CRITICALLY**

In this exercise, you will draw out the implications of theoretical frameworks or ideas and examine research results with an eye to their relevance for change. In an interesting article examining the reasons why men say they rape, Scully and Merolla (1985) introduced their research on 114 convicted rapists studied through personal interviews with a consideration of two very different explanations for why men rape: the psycho-dynamic and the socio-cultural models. These researchers describe the two models as follows:

the psychodynamic model	the socio-cultural model
Rape is an behavior which results from "idiosyncratic mental disease", usually accompanied by "uncontrollable sexual impulse" (p. 251). Male sexual aggression is regarded as unusual or strange (p. 252).	Rape is a learned behavior regarded as appropriate for males in a cultural context which supports male sexual aggression as a way to exert power and dominance. Rape is bolstered by stereotypes about women and by the belief that women like and want forced sex (pp. 252-3).

1. What do each of these models imply regarding the possibility of reducing the incidence of rape? That is, can you infer from each model that change is **possible**? Explain briefly.

    ( ) yes, in both   ( ) yes but only in the _____
    ( ) no   _____ model

    _____

    _____

    9
    Diana Scully and Joseph Merolla. "'Riding the Bull at Gilley's': Convicted Rapists Describe the Rewards of Rape." Social Problems. Vol. 32, No. 3 (February), pp. 251-263.

2.   Based on each theory, <u>where</u> should change
      efforts be targeted and <u>why</u>?

<u>Psychodynamic Model</u>   <u>Socio-cultural Model</u>

_____   _____

_____   _____

_____   _____

_____   _____

3.   Briefly comment on the likelihood of successful efforts
      in targeting the area you identified in question 2.
      Explain your answer briefly.

( ) highly likely ( ) somewhat likely ( ) not very likely

_____

_____

_____

_____

B.   **THINKING ABOUT THINKING**

      4.   Describe the thinking steps you took to answer
            questions 1 and 2.

      _____

      _____

      _____

      5.   What did you learn about the usefulness of theory
            and research from doing this exercise?

      _____

      _____

      _____

      _____

C. APPLYING WHAT YOU HAVE LEARNED

6. You are taking a course in which you must critique the interdisciplinary scholarly literature (e.g., sociological and psychological) on an important social topic: the social and psychological factors influencing excessive drinking among adolescents. You are expected to present the current state of social scientific thinking on this topic. An important part of your paper is identifying implications for change/applications (proposed, suggested, or implied) in each article and critically evaluating them and their likelihood of success.

   Based on what you have learned in this assignment, how would you approach identifying or drawing out and critiquing the implications of the theories and research you review?

   a. First, select **four empirical articles on this topic**-- two each from sociological and psychological journals. The articles you choose MUST contain, suggest, or imply intervention/change strategies on the topic.

   b. Provide the complete reference for each article you choose.

   c. Identify the **implications for change** in the theories used or in the research results reported on this topic in the spaces provided below each citation.

   d. Do an **overall assessment** of the implications for change identified, suggested, or implied in each article. Include comments on 1) the **target** of change identified (e.g., individuals, small group, organizational, cultural, institutional, or societal); interventions are in place; 2) the **time frame** likely to actually observe change, once the interventions are in place, and 3) the **priority** of particular intervention strategies-- that is an ordering of strategies from most important (to be addressed first) to less important.

Articles from Sociology Journals

#1 Citation: _____

_____

_____

Implications for Change/Applications: _____

_____

_____

_____

_____

Critical Assessment: _____

_____

_____

_____

_____

#2 Citation: _____

_____

_____

Implications for Change/Applications: _____

_____

_____

_____

_____

Critical Assessment: _____

_____

_____

_____

_____

Articles from Psychology Journals

#1 Citation: _____

_____

_____

Implications for Change/Applications: _____

_____

_____

_____

_____

Critical Assessment: _____

_____

_____

_____

_____

#2 Citation: _____

_____

_____

Implications for Change/Applications: _____

_____

_____

_____

_____

References

Babbie, E. 1998. <u>The Practice of Social Research</u>. 7th ed.
Belmont, CA: Wadsworth Publishing Company.

Eitzen, S. and M. Baca Zinn. 1998. <u>In Conflict and Order</u>.
8th ed. Boston: Allyn and Bacon.

Harel Z. et al. 1990. "Ethnicity and the Jewish Aged." <u>The Journal of
Aging and Judaism</u>. Vol. 5, No. 1 (Fall): 47-52.

Hernandez, D. 1995. <u>America's Children: Resources From
Family, Government, and the Economy</u>. New York: Russell
Sage Foundation.

Johnson, C. M., L. Miranda, A. Sherman, and J. D. Weill. 1991.
<u>Child Poverty in America</u>. Washington, D.C.: Children's
Defense Fund.

Kammeyer, K. C. W., G. Ritzer, and N. R. Yetman. 1997. <u>Sociology,
Experiencing Changing Societies</u>. Boston: Allyn and Bacon.

Merton, R. K. <u>Social Theory and Social Structure</u>. 1968. Expanded Edition. New York: The Free Press.

Mills, C. W. 1959. <u>The Sociological Imagination</u>. New York:
Oxford University Press.

Riordan, C. and A. Mazur. <u>Introductory Sociology Workbook</u>
(With Chip Software). New York: Harper and Row, 1988.

Rosenthal, R. and L. Jacobson. 1989. <u>Pygmalian in the Class-
room</u>. New York: Irvington Publishers.

Schutt, R. <u>Investigating the Social World</u>. 1996. Thousand
Oaks, CA: Pine Forge Press.

Scully, D. and J. Marolla. 1985. "'Riding the Bull at Gilley's':
Convicted Rapists Describe the Rewards of Rape." <u>Social
Problems</u>. Vol. 32, No. 3 (February): 251-63.

Soldo, B. J. and E. Agree. 1988. "America's Elderly." <u>Popula-
tion Bulletin</u> 43.

Treas, J. "Older Americans in the 1990s and Beyond." <u>Population
Bulletin</u> 50.

<u>Time Magazine</u>. 1997. July 21.

U. S. Bureau of the Census. 1995b. <u>Statistical Abstract of the
United States</u>. Washington, D. C.: U. S. Government Print-
ing Office.

<u>U. S. News and World Report</u>. 1994. (October)